A BOOK BY
SYLVAIN LABS

THE DOTS: VOL. 7

The inner workings of influence
for brands and institutions in the modern era.

Inspired by real-life social experiments conducted in
secrecy over 2 years. This is what we learned.

CONTENTS

Section Three
APPLYING INFLUENCE

Section Four
WRAPPING IT ALL UP

PREFACE

A WORD FROM ALAIN SYLVAIN
FOUNDER & CEO

Writing a book can be an audacious and arrogant endeavor. It's fraught with condescension and entitlement and, increasingly, it's not that hard to do. This book, The Dots, didn't have to answer to an editor or a publishing calendar. It doesn't have a built-in audience, and it isn't riding the wave of some celebrity endorsement. It probably won't get translated or win some award. At best it will serve as some sort of shelf art, and at worst it will be ignored and forgotten after the first five sentences of the preface.

Quite simply, we decided to write a book. So we wrote a book. Does the world really need another book? There are tons of books. We quickly learned that there are even tons of books about writing books.

We executed this narcissistic fantasy and, what do you know, here it is.

But it's worth noting a few things. We at Sylvain Labs, for better or worse, document and share our ideas all the time. It's actually the only thing we do. We help big companies rethink their products and brands, and we do that by documenting and sharing our ideas.

Also, this was really, really hard. It took years. It didn't take years because we researched one topic exhaustively over time – it took years because we were easily distracted and demotivated. But again, somehow, here it is.

To be fair, "we" didn't write the book as much as Joey Camire wrote the book. His idea to take all of our learning and package it this way was inspired. Not only did he galvanize the project, he committed to writing (and drawing) the vast majority.

This would not have happened in the first place if Frank Cooper III hadn't challenged us with questions like, "What is influence?" "How are we influenced?" "Why are we influenced?"

And his challenge makes sense. After all, the question of influence is at the core of everything we do – whether voluntarily or involuntarily. We are constantly influenced by others, by media, by our perceptions and experiences. And if we can understand influence, we may understand humanity itself. It's also really interesting to think about influence through different lenses – as the influenced or as the influencer, for example.

We hope you enjoy the book, and we look forward to hearing your reaction.

SECTION ONE
INTRODUCTION TO INFLUENCE

Chapter One
Everything Is Influence

Chapter Two
Thinking Influence

CHAPTER ONE
EVERYTHING IS INFLUENCE

Influence — the idea of impacting the objects, people, and ideas that surround us — is as fundamental to the human experience as any idea can be. Literally, the fundamental forces of physics are all related to the ways in which objects influence each other.

But when taken in the context of how we live our lives — how we make decisions, whom we choose to believe, and how we build our worldviews — influence is unavoidably entangled. In so many ways, we are just the product of our interactions with the people who surrounded us, the way they change our own view of things, and, in turn, how our own behaviors and actions bend and alter the way they see things.

It begins at the moment of birth — the way we're held, washed, spanked, all begin to influence us in subtle ways.

As we grow, the ways we're parented, taught, befriended, or bullied all create deep influences on who we become and how we behave. But what is even more compelling about influence is that our lack of behavior can have just as much influence on others as our behaviors themselves. In this way, influence is a constant. It exists because of us, but it exists independently of us as well. It is a constant push and pull on all the people we're connected to.

When you text a friend about an amazing meal you just enjoyed, you're creating a positive impression of that restaurant in her mind. When you wear your favorite band's T-shirt, you're affecting a person you pass on the street, convincing him that he might not like that band, because he doesn't like the way you look. Even the absence of something can act as an influence. By not discussing a particular public event, either by choice or simply by being unaware, we're sending a message to others about the level of import that event has. Absolutely everything you do, every single decision, creates some ripple out in the world. And the more influence you possess as an individual, the greater the amplitude of the ripples your decisions make.

If you don't believe this, watch the simple banalities that celebrities engage in that can create massive tidal waves of change through culture as a whole — see Ashton Kutcher's trucker hats, Kanye West's drop-crotch ninja pants, Kate Middleton's fascinators, or Kylie Jenner's lip challenge. These influences can be positive or negative — as often as celebrity culture gives us Toms Shoes, it gives us UGGs. But these giant and rapid waves of influence don't come only from the wildly famous. In fact, sometimes the most famous are the last to jump on the bandwagon. The ALS Ice Bucket Challenge is a great example of the media and famous people as hangers-on to a phenomenon that was happening independently of them.

In examples like the Ice Bucket Challenge, we begin to see, in stark relief, that fame and influence are not necessarily synonymous concepts — moments when we realize the importance of understanding influence as a discrete concept. And if this thing — entity, idea, concept, force, however you choose to view it — is constantly in action all around us, there is most certainly value in attempting to understand it.

It was this question, "What is influence, and how does it work?" that sent us on a 2-year journey — and so *The Dots* was born.

INTRODUCING
THE DOTS

Since the birth of Sylvain Labs, through the large variety of our clients and projects, we've been asked one question more than any others.

It's come in a variety of iterations — "Who are the cool kids?" "Who is influencing the cool kids?" "What the hell is influence anyway?" "Why can't we be cool kids?" From the persistence of this question, we understood that there wasn't a good answer out there. We also realized that while we felt like we intuitively understood influence, we didn't have an answer that satisfied our own desire to make sense of the world, and that really bugged us.

Over the past 2 years at Sylvain Labs we became obsessed with the idea of influence. Not the evil genius, Machiavellian sort of obsession — in the way that you encounter a problem that you just can't get out of your head, a problem that begins to infiltrate all of your unoccupied moments. We've investigated subcultures around the world first-hand, we've explored emerging trends and the way those ideas are disseminated, and we've documented the lives of people who have experienced the swell and collapse that influence can have on someone's life. We've hung out with the cool kids, and we've hung out with the nerds.

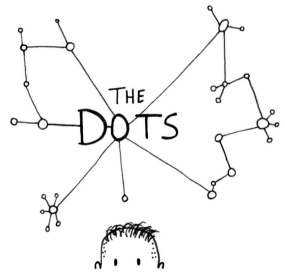

Through these clandestine immersions and public exposures, we've started to develop our own theories about the ways that influence works, or at the very least the ways in which we can understand influence better. Because there is something that surrounds us, that we don't see, that we obscure behind the idea of "influence," that is so much more massive than we tend to give it credit for.

This obsession has taken on a project name — The Dots — because when you give something a name, it becomes real and begins to take on a life of its own. The name is twofold in nature. First, it is about our quest to connect the dots, which explain how influence works. Second, it was born of our hope to uncover the distributed network of influence that births and beheads ideas, a network that quietly informs us of what we like and what we don't. The nodes in that distributed network, the dots, is one aspect of what we've spent the last 2 years searching for. Our search, it turns out, was a lot more like that of Ponce De Leon than that of Marco Polo — no fountain of influence to be found, but a lot of discovery along the way.

This book is a series of demonstrations and explanations of how we've begun, as a company, to codify our own perspective on what influence is and the ways in which it operates in the world around us. This isn't a scientific exploration (though it might contain some science). Instead, it is a whole lot of intuition mixed with research and examples. It's as much a philosophical thesis as it is an anecdotal record of our interactions with the world.

More than anything, this book is meant to be fun. The type of book we like to read. Learning something new and meaningful doesn't have to come with a starched pair of pleated, tapered, cuffed khaki pants and a sedative. Unless you're into that kind of thing. In the immortal words of Pretty Toney, "Y'all smart dumb cats need to wisen up!" We're just here to make sure it's a good time.

Enjoy.

CHAPTER TWO
THINKING INFLUENCE

The goal of this book is to share the ways in which we've come to view influence. With that said, it's important to note a few things on what you're about to read.

Although what you've already read and the sections that follow are things we believe to be true, this isn't a silver bullet. It should also be stated that finding the silver bullet has never been our goal — mostly because silver bullets are bullshit, as imaginary as werewolves (sorry #TeamJacob).

Instead, it is our hope to create a sort of Sapir-Whorf effect — to create a clear enough understanding of influence that the idea can exist completely in our minds in such a way that we can apply it with deftness and ease. If law schools attempt to teach people to "think the law," we want to be able to "think influence." However, in order to get started, there are two important things to note.

NOTE ONE
THE IMPORTANCE OF INTUITION

The difference between the law and influence* is that the law has an enormous amount of reference material and discrete information.

*The other difference is the litany of great
jokes about lawyers

So much is codified, so many boundaries have been set. Influence, however, is immensely nebulous in nature. People have tried to define metrics for influence for a long time, and although there is likely some correlation between an algorithm like Klout or Q Score and real-world influence, the number of factors that are involved in determining influence in the real world are well outside the confines of any algorithm on the market today.

For this reason, a huge amount of intuition, empathy, and gut is required to identify and employ influence. There is something innately human about understanding and predicting how other people will behave that is inextricable from this subject. It's only logical that intuition should be involved. People understand other people on a subconscious level. This is why we aren't constantly running into each other when walking down a crowded sidewalk — we're doing tons of calculations about each others' movements, intentions, speeds, trajectories, and terrible fashion decisions without ever consciously thinking about it.

More and more, science is uncovering the immense ability people have to take in information through all of our senses and parse it in ways outside of what we might normally consider analytical thinking. One great example of this is what NASA fellow Robert Alexander is doing with data being captured from the sun. Instead of forcing scientists to pore over more data than they can possibly handle, Alexander has embarked on the "sonification" of data. By attaching different notes and tones to distinct types of data, he's allowed people to listen to the sun and to process immense data sets through a much more intuitive means. The result is that scientists listening to his sonified data have been able to make breakthroughs in the behavior of the sun by identifying anomalous fluctuations in the music.

The idea here is that we should embrace our gut as a first line of interpreting influence. If anything, over the past 2 years of our experimentation, this idea of the necessary intuition involved in understanding influence has become more and more apparent. Instead of avoiding the conversation about how messy this is (*this* being the human factor), we want to use it as an asset. All great leaps in science demand an artistically inspired perspective, a leap of insight that comes from somewhere beyond the pen and paper, beyond computers and algorithms. Why should the science of influence be any different?

If this is a skill, then some people should have a natural ability to see and understand influence better than others. Everyone can improve at it, but some people will always stand out.

NOTE TWO
A NON-ZERO-SUM GAME

It's important for us to note that we're thinking about influence in a completely organic and socially accepted context.

We're not talking about coercion, bribery, or fear mongering. For this reason, much of the influence we discuss is a non-zero-sum game, often in the positive direction. Without going completely *A Beautiful Mind* on influence, what we mean by a positive non-zero-sum game is that both parties win — it's a win-win scenario. It's very easy to perceive influence as an inherently sneaky or subversive thing — that it's manipulative by nature to change the way another person thinks or acts — but this bias fails to look at the entire picture objectively.

When someone chooses to initiate, change, or amplify an existing behavior based on the influence of another, it can be assumed that they are doing this for some perceived positive reward. If one mom tells another mom a story about an experience she had and the second mom takes her story into consideration in future decision making, regardless of whether it's adding or subtracting a behavior, the reason the second mom is changing her behavior is to achieve some perceived reward. The same goes for a teenager who mimics a celebrity — they're adopting a behavior, that is to say being influenced, because they believe the change might come with some amount of social cachet, or could possibly be a clearer expression of something they're already thinking or feeling. This is a positive exchange. Everybody wins, even if the rewards are not apples to apples.

	+1 "YOU WIN"	−1 "YOU LOSE"
+1 "I WIN"	+2 "WIN – WIN"	0 "ZERO SUM"
−1 "I LOSE"	0 "ZERO SUM"	−2 "LOSE – LOSE"

The reason that both of these examples are non-zero-sum is that in both cases the influencer benefits, as well the influenced. In the case of the mom passing on a helpful anecdote, she becomes seen as a knowledgeable pillar in the community and establishes credibility. Although the increase in power in her community may be negligible from that single instance, repeating this type of interaction over time grows her ability to affect change in ways that fit with her values or agenda. Each instance takes her one step closer to the day when she'll be publicly recognized as the single greatest mom of all time, or the president of the PTA. Whichever comes first.

In the case of the celebrity who influences the teenager, the teenager adopts a behavior to co-opt some of the celebrity's attributes (intentionally or not). But the celebrity benefits as well. In almost all cases, celebrities use their influence to sell something — be it their own creative product like movies or music, or something more direct like selling their likeness to companies to help market products. Every time a person adopts a behavior from a celebrity, that person is also emotionally migrating that celebrity toward "in-group" status, meaning that the influenced person views himself as part of the same cohort, team, or type of person. We trust people whom we consider "in-group" and are dramatically more likely to take their advice in purchasing decisions. Every instance of influence increases the celebrity's ability to sell whatever it is they're selling that day, and thereby make them money. While in this example the benefits are different, trading status for money, they are both positive. And so a Kim Kardashian is born.

The point is, influence isn't necessarily a bad thing, or at least it's not intrinsically bad. In fact, the entire social contract we engage in as citizens of our homes, offices, cities, states, and countries, is grounded in influence. It's a force that can move nations to both positive and negative outcomes, and it shouldn't be viewed with any type of qualitative modifiers when discussed in its purest sense. Influence is a tool like any other tool, it can be used for both good and evil.

However, we implore you to use it for good, because, despite the appeals of Billy Joel, the good don't always die young.

SECTION TWO
CONCEPTUALIZING INFLUENCE

CHAPTER THREE
GRAVITY AND THE FABRIC OF INFLUENCE

When we talk about influence, what we're really talking about is the impact that one person, idea, or institution has on the decision making of others around them (without coercion or a really big stick).

An individual's influence can be seen in the effect she has on her immediate social circles, but the depth and intensity of influence can obviously move well beyond a person's immediate connections. In fact, it's when influence starts to spread out into further and further connections, six degrees of separation and so on, that it takes on entirely new proportions. (Incidentally, this is where you'll find Kevin Bacon.)

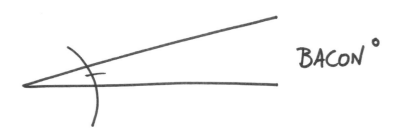

BACON°

USING PHYSICS TO MODEL A THEORY OF INFLUENCE

We've begun to realize that it's more effective to view influence in three dimensions than as a nebulous concept.

In our three-dimensional model, influence is analogous to gravity and its effects on the fabric of space-time. The size and mass of a celestial body can be considered as equivalent to the size and mass of a person's influence, because in both cases, as the amount of mass or influence increases, the effect an object or person has on the bodies that surround it increases. In the case of a planet, that effect might be seen in the orbit of a communications satellite or a moon. In the case of people, that effect of influence is seen in the orbits of the people whose decisions are impacted by the influencer they gravitate toward.

In this model, the larger the person's influence, the more he warps the area around him. In the case of gravity, objects warp the fabric of space-time in relationship to their mass; in the case of influence, we can call this the "fabric of influence." The more influence a person has, the deeper the depression she creates in the fabric of influence, which starts to affect people further and further out from herself. For gravity, this depression is called a *Gravity Well*. For influence we'll call this depression in the fabric an *Influence Well*.

Every person, idea, and one-hit-wonder creates its own distinct Influence Well, in the same way that every planet, star, and black hole creates its own distinct gravity well. In the case of gravity, objects are drawn down to the bottom of the gravity well toward the object creating it. In the case of influence, decisions are drawn down to the bottom of the Influence Well, toward the person or idea creating it. If a decision makes it to the bottom of an Influence Well, that decision gets directly influenced by whatever is creating that Influence Well.

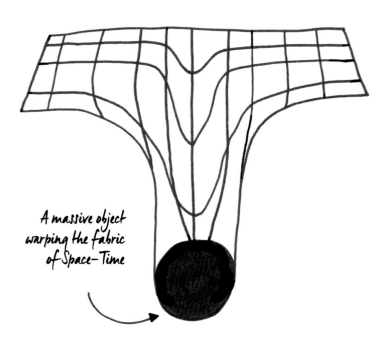

A massive object warping the fabric of Space-Time

ALLOWING THE COOL KIDS TO DEMONSTRATE

The difference between visualizing gravity and influence arises when you consider the stratification of arenas where influence can take place.

For example, take someone like Michelle Phan, a woman who has built an extremely impressive amount of fame from her YouTube video tutorials on the best ways to apply makeup and other beauty products. For those trapped in a coma for all of 2014, Michelle Phan was one of the key highlights of YouTube's 2014 media blitz, which saw hundreds of versions of her face festooning billboards across the country. Her influence is almost completely exclusive to health and beauty products — a single layer of influence — but her impact in this arena is extremely deep. She sits atop the pinnacle of the world she plays in — the Martha Stewart of makeup, the Beyoncé of beauty supplies.

Consider this against the fame and influence of Tavi Gevinson, the young media powerhouse of Style Rookie and Rookie Mag, and newly minted Broadway actor. Gevinson is massively influential in the world of fashion, especially for teen girls. She is so influential, in fact, that she graced the cover of *New York Magazine's* 2014 Fall Fashion issue — no small feat for even the most veteran figures in fashion. But where

Gevinson's influence begins to depart from Phan's, and to take on greater texture, is with the addition of the other strata of influence that she impacts. Gevinson's Rookie Mag is an online lifestyle magazine for young women that covers topics ranging from how to write a novel to music, jobs, relationships, and more. Rookie has become a sort of demonstration of the precocious identity of modern young women, and a source of empowerment for teen girls across the country. It is this drive to fight against being defined by a single thing — a push against the one-dimensional definitions that the media have placed on women of the past — that starts to demonstrate how Gevinson's influence takes a wider-reaching hold.

This is what separates Phan's and Gevinson's styles of influence — the diversity of areas where they're influential and the number and types of people drawn into their Influence Wells.

While Michelle Phan may not present her fans with videos on how to handle sexual harassment at work or how to write a college essay, her fans are probably not turning to her for that kind of information. She's a resource for beauty. However, it seems completely natural when Gevinson's Rookie Mag offers advice for young women on these topics and more. Fans want Tavi to bring the broad view. They want her to explore new areas. Certainly there are limits to her range, but they probably relate more to the amount of content devoted to a given topic rather than to the topic itself. Fans wouldn't want Rookie to turn into a health website, but if it covered something like "What It Was Like to Get an STI" or "How to Talk to Your Gyno" or even "Living with OCD," they'd be interested. That's because these are stories about the human condition, and Tavi has the latitude to go there and still remain influential.

LOOKING BEYOND THE NUMBERS

If we were looking at this comparison from a purely statistical perspective, Michelle Phan wins hands down. Tyson vs. Frazier. At the time of this writing, Michelle Phan has roughly 660K followers on Twitter to Gevinson's roughly 300k. Phan has 1.7 million Instagram followers to Gevinson's 214K. From this perspective, there is no contest. But anyone who works in media knows that reach alone isn't the be-all and end-all.

When imagined in this three-dimensional model, the depth that Phan reaches in one stratum of social influence may be deeper than that of any of Gevinson's — for example, Phan's say in makeup and beauty products may carry more weight than Gevinson's in fashion. But when you compound all the layers in which Gevinson carries influence — fashion, music, culture, art, lifestyle, etc. — you begin to understand why her overall social influence may be equal to or greater than Phan's in terms of the number of decisions she has an impact on, even if it's across fewer total individuals.

This of course is just an example — Michelle Phan could be the most influential woman in America, although probably not — but it helps to demonstrate how influence has texture and needs to be considered in a more holistic sense than simply looking at the number of Twitter or Instagram followers an individual has accrued. This nuance asks us to examine why we bring people into our lives, what motivates us to allow them occupancy in our attention space, and the ways in which we construct our mental images of them.

This way of visualizing influence gives us a model to begin to demonstrate the full context. It allows us to cut to the core of what influence is — the impact of decision making — and begin to compare one individual's influence to another's.

Now that we've shown the model from a high level, we can dive into the individual characteristics of how people and ideas create Influence Wells, and how we can build them with intention.

CHAPTER FOUR
BUILDING INFLUENCE WELLS

By this point a nagging question may have slowly crept in.

Beyond the simple benefit of being able to better understand and analyze influence through a useful metaphor, how can we apply this model to create change in the present, as opposed to just analyzing influence in the past? Transitioning from the theoretical perspective to application is a challenge that all, from physicists to social scientists, face. It's the pubescent period of an idea, full of pimples and unsure of its place in the world.

Using celebrities is hardly a new strategy for influencing others. Marketers and policy makers have employed it successfully for quite a long time. Results may vary, but when choosing someone who has influence in the arena you're trying to impact, celebrity involvement often moves the needle. One key problem with using major celebrities is that their influence comes at a (considerable) price — unless of course it's a cause they're willing to donate to free of charge, but good luck with that. In a world no longer composed of only two separate states of influence — a lot or none — it's worth understanding how to apply this new theory of Influence Wells to everyday circumstances.

FOCUS, DEPTH, AND BREADTH

An Influence Well has three key attributes: focus, depth, and breadth. These three features are based on things happening in the real world, and although they may be the product of wildly complex systems and network interactions, they are real and tangible. If this is true, then we should be able to construct Influence Wells of our own based on applying these ideas.

FOCUS

Focus deals with how clearly and singularly an idea or person is able to directly connect their message to decision-making moments. Focus is the difference between intention and action. If influence is the measure of how many decisions something creates or changes, when constructing an Influence Well there is an obvious imperative to be as clear as possible.

In the case of this model, focus represents the permeability of an Influence Well's walls. If you think about the very bottom of the Influence Well as the moment when a decision is made, focus is what allows a person to be drawn to the bottom of the Influence Well without shooting out the sides before making it there. The more focus, the less permeable the wall of the Influence Well, and the more likely that someone's behaviors are affected. To that end, you can think about big decisions as having more "mass," and therefore influencing those decisions requires a larger well. Celebrities in a popularity contest, chasing cool for the sake of it, have the privilege of being ambiguously influential. But for people setting out to influence others toward a specific objective, laser focus is imperative. What behavior are you changing or creating? How will you articulate that?

If you're trying to influence someone, you need to be able to say how. Buy this. Don't buy that. Eat this. Don't eat that. Share this. Watch that. Go here. Read this. Listen to that. All behaviors. All need to be explicitly expressed.

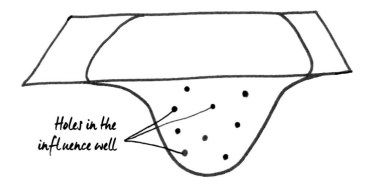

Holes in the influence well

More focus, less permeability. Get it? Maybe an example will help. Stephen Colbert, arguably a contender for the most influential person in America over the past decade, has consistently found ways to not only build but to experiment with the influence of his show. His brand of political satire and pseudo shock-jock persona has initiated a maelstrom of social experiments and crowd swells over the past decade. So much of what he's done is a clear demonstration of influence, but nothing demonstrates the laser focus of an Influence Well better than his exchange with his fans about the naming competition for NASA's expansion of the ISS.

In 2009, NASA ran a competition to name the Node 3 add-on to the International Space Station. On his March 3, 2009 episode, Stephen Colbert threw down the gauntlet — he told his viewers "You are officially mobilized to name that space station after me." From there he clearly outlined exactly what he wanted people to do, "So heroes, go to colbertnation.com, then follow the link to the NASA website, select suggest your own, and type in the word 'Colbert'."

There is no ambiguity in his message, it is the picture of focus. He is an influencer who employed his influence to create a behavior, and in outlining the behavior he was creating, he left nothing to the imagination. In this way, there were no holes in his Influence Well, no place to fall out of. Ultimately, his fans won the contest for him, but NASA declined to name the node after him, opting instead for Tranquility. However, in an effort to extend an olive branch, they named the treadmill that would be placed in Tranquility the "Combined Operational Load Bearing External Resistance Treadmill," or "C.O.L.B.E.R.T." for short. Although it was a consolation prize, the C.O.L.B.E.R.T. was still a great victory for Stephen, because NASA made the point in their press release that they don't typically name their hardware after living human beings.

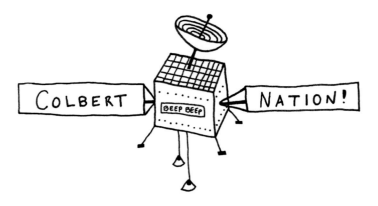

DEPTH

The easiest way to think about depth is as a positive correlation between the height of an Influence Well and the desire to act on a particular behavior. In clearer terms, the deeper the well, the stronger the influence to act. This description explains what depth represents, but in order to really understand the motivation to act when being influenced, we have to have a higher-level conversation about motivation in general. Why does anyone do anything? Or, to quote Carl Sagan, "If you wish to make an apple pie from scratch, you must first invent the universe."

In Chapter 2, we discussed how influence is a non-zero-sum game — that both the influencer and the influenced can get something positive from their interaction. For that reason, it's important to think of each behavior created in an Influence Well as an exchange. On the other side of the action there is a reward, either perceived or real, that the person being influenced believes they are getting from the exchange. And that reward doesn't have to be monetary or physical; emotional rewards are very real. The greater the draw toward a reward, the more likely that someone will act, and the deeper the Influence Well.

It's important not to lose sight of the transactionality of influence when you are building an Influence Well. There are many reasons why someone like Justin Timberlake is influential; he's a legitimate triple threat. But it all boils down to the fact that interacting with Justin delivers a consistently positive reward. Whether this is through perennially high-quality music and performances, or just through the reward of seeing his dashing good looks, we get something positive every time we interact with him. This is why *The 20/20 Experience* was the best-selling album of 2013, a very direct result of his influence. It's also probably a big part of why we saw a proliferation of short-sides-long-top haircuts on men in 2013 and 2014 as well. This means that something that made people feel good at the barbershop, that undeniable feeling of cool after a fresh cut, also gets tied back to Justin's Influence Well.

So how do we make sure that Influence Wells have that same level of depth without having the uncanny ability to bring sexy back? In the case of Stephen Colbert, it was about making people feel part of a group (the Colbert Nation) that made a mark on history. In the case of Justin Timberlake, it's about that pitter-patter he puts in our hearts and pants, and those aren't easily recreatable feelings. How can we ensure depth of an Influence Well when we're dealing with the boring aspects of everyday life?

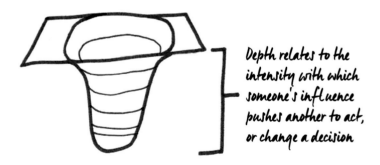

Depth relates to the intensity with which someone's influence pushes another to act, or change a decision

There is hardly anything more banal than credit cards. They possess the emotional appeal of bran flakes and wet blankets. Yet credit card companies have figured out a way to create huge amounts of influence through a system that has convinced us that interacting with them is in our best interest — points.

Credit card loyalty programs, while being highly nebulous and arcane systems, have convinced card holders that if at the point of transaction they use their credit card instead of cash, they're getting something extra out of the deal. It's this belief in a reward that drives people to choose their cards over cash if everything else is equal. The reality is that unless people pay off their bill right away, the credit card companies are getting the better end of the deal, but the perception of reward is enough to affect a huge number of buying decisions every month. This means that for many people, at the moment of transaction, the Influence Well for credit cards is significant enough to change their behavior.

The reason that credit card companies' points systems create deep Influence Wells isn't based on any deep emotional feeling, it's an extremely logical and rational perception of reward. And this is important; you may not always be able to create a connection with people in the way that Justin Timberlake does, and that shouldn't be the expectation — the man brought sexy back, for God's sake. But when you realize that influence still boils down to a transaction, you don't need to bring sexy back to be influential — you just need the right incentive. It's economics, my dear Watson.

BREADTH

The final characteristic of Influence Wells is their breadth. Breadth is (thankfully) the most straightforward aspect of the model. Breadth, for all intents and purposes, is equivalent to the reach of the message. It's that easy. This doesn't, however, reduce its significance, because you can't influence the decisions of people your message hasn't reached.

This aspect of Influence Wells is hugely important when contemplating building new ones, because influence can be aggregated from many individuals into one giant well around an idea, cause, or initiative. Imagine the individual Influence Wells of 100 people, all having different depths, breadths, and even focus as it relates to different ideas. But if all of those people are speaking or acting toward a single message, their individual Influence Wells can be added together to form the greater Influence Well of the idea or cause in question.

There is a quintessential example that clearly demonstrates this idea. Live Aid.

Live Aid was organized in the summer of 1985 by two British musicians, Bob Geldof and Midge Ure, to raise money and awareness about a debilitating famine afflicting Ethiopia. Live Aid was their second foray into aggregating Influence Wells. Their first was recording the song "Do They Know It's Christmas" with musicians like Boy George, Sting, George Michael, Bono, Phil Collins, Duran Duran, Kool and The Gang, and more. Following the success of "Do They Know It's Christmas?," they set out to do it even bigger. The concert brought together what must have felt like all of the most famous musicians in the world. Looking at the set list is like a walk through the Rock N' Roll Hall of Fame. Names at the UK concert included Sade, Phil Collins, Sting, U2, Duran Duran, Elton John, Queen, Paul McCartney, David Bowie, and more. At the U.S. concert there were The Beach Boys, Crosby Stills & Nash, The Four Tops, Run DMC, Black Sabbath, Billy Ocean, REO Speedwagon, The Pretenders, Madonna, The Cars, Neil Young, Tom Petty and the Heartbreakers, Eric Clapton, Hall & Oates, and more.

Some of these individual musical acts alone were influential enough to sell out the venues where Live Aid was being held (Wembley Stadium and John F. Kennedy Stadium), but the sheer power of their collective influence was enough to hold almost half the world in rapt attention. The result was undeniable. The Live Aid concert, which had originally set its fundraising goal at $1 million, raised over $140 million. The concert also set the all-time broadcast record, with estimates placing global viewership at over 1.9 billion people.

By aggregating the ability of all of these individuals to influence certain groups' behaviors, Live Aid dramatically expanded the breadth of the Influence Well directed at getting donations to help bring relief to the Ethiopian countryside. In one day's concentrated influence, they were able to raise the 2015 equivalent of over $300 million.

CHAPTER FIVE
INFLUENCERS ARE MODERN GODS

The 90s was a decade lousy with strange obsessions and odd cultural memes that had a tendency to permeate society on a large scale — things like Pogs, Beanie Babies, Jonathan Taylor Thomas, neon anything, snap bracelets, Starter jackets, Tamagotchis, Tickle Me Elmo, Furbies, and the list goes on.

But among these bits of pop culture nostalgia exists a perfect example of influence in action — a bracelet that adorned the wrists of teens and preteens across the country with four simple letters on it — WWJD.

Although bracelets have had many viral moments over the years — for example the 2000s had their own bracelet craze in those yellow Livestrong bracelets — what separates the WWJD bracelets is the message behind the letters. For those who didn't experience the craze, WWJD stands for "What Would Jesus Do?" The bracelet asks, if not implores, its wearers to consider Jesus in every decision they make, allowing Jesus (the idea) to influence all of their conscious conclusions.

Now regardless of one's stance on religion or Christianity, Jesus has hardly been hurting for influence — he's been influencing minds and nations for centuries. But based on the model we've begun to outline, what these bracelets did, at least for the time they existed, was to dramatically increase the number of decisions that Jesus had a part in. For this period, if the bracelets played their intended function (and there were plenty of proselytizing teens), Jesus' Influence Well took on new proportions. According to a conservative estimate of bracelet sales, one corporation sold 16 million bracelets by the year 2000. However, some estimates place sales at over 50 million bracelets across the United States in the '90s. This means that if any of these teens took this bracelet seriously, if they considered the question "What Would Jesus Do?" on a semi-regular basis, we can say that Jesus had an increase in influence in the 1990s based on bracelets.

This idea was not created with the WWJD bracelet. People have used artifacts to increase the influence they have on each other for centuries. The wedding band is a great example of ways that we choose to influence the behavior of others around us. For the partners it serves as a constant reminder to consider each other in the daily decisions they make, regardless of whether it's something banal or something more serious like fidelity. For others outside the partnership, it serves as a universal communication of unavailability (at least in theory). This reminder is influence. It is a dramatic warping of the fabric of influence, if only for the one individual who is being reminded. However, rings also work on larger scales. Alumni of universities choose to wear class rings to remind themselves of their loyalty to their school and the camaraderie they have with classmates. Freemasons wear rings as a signifier of their membership in a secret club. They act as reminders of in-group status and the expectations that membership carries — be it to a university, a Masonic temple, or the person waiting for you to come home and watch Netflix.

MIRROR NEURONS FOR THE WIN

The reason all of this can happen, and maybe noncoercive influence in general, is due to a few cells in our brains, called *mirror neurons*. To grossly simplify, mirror neurons are cells located in several parts of the brain that enable the empathic abilities of human beings. Mirror neurons allow us to adopt the perspective of others, in both physical and emotional terms. Mirror neurons make us cringe when someone else bangs their shin, and make us sad when we see others crying. It's this ability to remove ourselves from our own situations and try to adopt the perspective of another that fuels influence. This is how we can ask the question "What Would Jesus Do?" or what any god or prophet would do, or want from us. What would Allah do? What would Buddha do? What would Kanye do?

"It is difficult to overstate the importance of understanding mirror neurons and their function. They may well be central to social learning, imitation, and the cultural transmission of skills and attitudes— perhaps even of the pressed-together sound clusters we call words. By hyperdeveloping the mirror-neuron system, evolution in effect turned culture into the new genome."

- *V.S. Ramachandran*

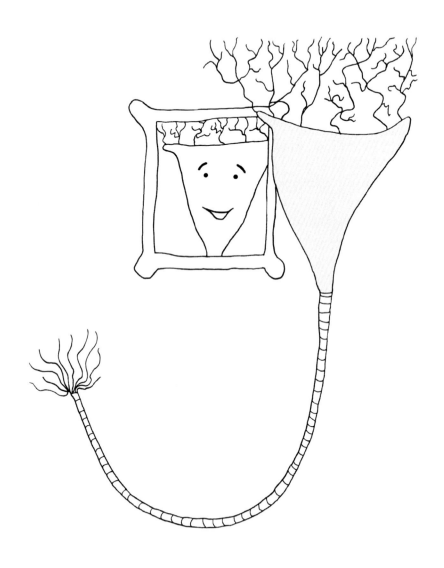

When we ask ourselves these questions, what we're really doing is accessing a model of these gods that we've constructed in our minds, fundamentally a God Algorithm, and using it to predict how the god would behave in a given situation. We use empathy to help us make decisions based on how we predict those wiser, smarter, or more divine individuals would behave. Employing our predictions, we choose the behaviors that align us with their approach to the world. This is influence: predicting what someone would do, or want us to do, and doing it.

In terms of this model, God is just a giant depression in the fabric of influence. An Influence Well of epic proportions. Crass, maybe, but conceptually accurate.

ALGORITHM | ˈalgəˌriT͟Həm |

noun   a process or set of rules to be followed in calculations or other problem-solving operations, especially by a computer

When we start to explore influence and the ways the fabric of influence warps around real people in the world, the construct is no different than with the gods we referenced earlier. All of the people we look to and call "influencers" or "influentials"— their real power is derived from the models that everyday people create in their minds to represent these "influencers." Essentially, the most influential people in the world are really just heuristics, elaborate flowchart residing in people's minds that they choose to deploy in given situations. A tool, a device to pull down from the metaphorical shelf, to help work through a situation.

This is how influence extends beyond the boundaries of explicitly stated suggestions into unique scenarios that our influencers never discussed or even considered, but that their influence is generalized to. If a young girl asks herself how Beyoncé would handle a conflict with her boyfriend, a unique and specific situation that Beyoncé never could have discussed, this young girl is calling upon all of her experience with and exposure to Beyoncé to generalize to an extremely personal scenario. She is running the Beyoncé Algorithm.

This Goop example illustrates this point.

THE GOOP ALGORITHM

Gwyneth Paltrow has, over the past several years, become the de facto voice of the all-natural, organic, raw world view. Her growing media empire at Goop has become influential as a lifestyle outlet for conscientious consumers with a bent toward the holistic. Goop gives recommendations on everything from underwear and fashion items to healthy meal recipes and alternatives. They've even gone as far as trying to reinvent the way that we look at and talk about divorce with their piece about "conscious uncoupling."

What makes Gwyneth and Goop so interesting is the clarity of the broad spanning set of rules they've outlined. People have a very clear idea of how and why they believe that Gwyneth is doing the things she is doing.

Although they may not always agree with all of her decisions, they've decided that they agree with the model that she is using to make those decisions. So when women across the country who want to take a more holistic approach to their lives begin to make decisions about what to do, buy, or believe, they employ the "Gwyneth Algorithm." They take a step back and ask themselves, consciously or unconsciously, "what would Gwyneth do" given the circumstances that they find themselves in. In this way Gwyneth is influencing their behavior and decisions in circumstances she's potentially never discussed, because she has become something far greater than a person — Gwyneth Paltrow is the God of Holistic Living.

Of course, it goes without saying that she is also influential in a more direct sense — "buy this, not that." But the point is that when someone like Gwyneth transcends from being just a credible product pusher to a "god," large numbers of people begin to use a model of the influencer to adjust their behaviors in ways and situations outside her actual experience or explicit advice.

And it's not just Gwyneth, there are countless other modern deities — Oprah, Ellen, Rush, Barack, J-Law, LeBron — the list goes on. These are the people whose warp on the fabric of influence has become so great that it has moved beyond them as individuals. The models of them we hold in our heads are influencing our decisions without the influencers needing to do anything. Essentially, these gods have become vessels for us to attach complex sets of ideas, rules, and morals to so that we have them at our disposal.

This idea, that influencers and celebrities are algorithms we hold in our heads distinct from who these people really are as individuals, demonstrates how influence is a social construct. The public decides which people will become famous and which will not, the product of supply and demand demonstrated through media companies' metrics like page views and shares. It shows that we need these people, influencers, to help us navigate the world around us, to help bring form to ideas in the ether that feel important to the world we're living in.

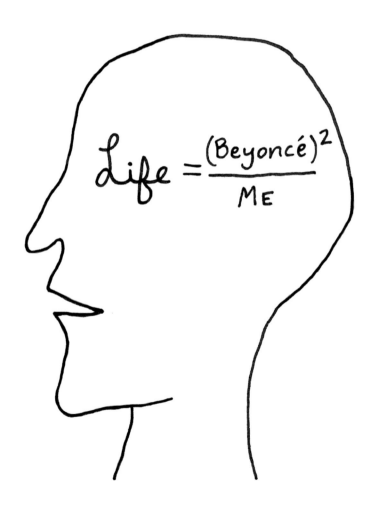

$$\textit{Life} = \frac{(Beyoncé)^2}{ME}$$

This is why, as a culture, we love Taylor Swift so much. She is the algorithm that reminds us of the importance of humility, honesty, and that it's ok to not pretend to be somebody you're not. When young people, and maybe some of us older folks too, glom onto Taylor Swift's heartfelt year in review "Thank You" videos, what we're really doing is expanding the complexity of our Taylor algorithm. So if her fans ever find some success of their own, they can use her as a reference that it's right to give back to the people who helped them find that success.

In many ways, what we're talking about is an old idea with a new skin — "role models." The difference here is that instead of being something that happens only in some short critical window during our childhood, these algorithms are dynamic mental constructs that we add to, adjust, and build on throughout our entire lives. The stable of algorithms we choose to keep in our head is our toolkit for navigating our everyday lives and society in general. They're what give us a sense of security in the decisions we make, and they add heft and tangibility to our ideas.

To be honest, the title of this chapter, "Influencers Are Modern Gods," is intentionally provocative, but that shouldn't negate the validity of the metaphor. Throughout much of history, gods have been these monolithic constructs used to help individuals make decisions in one direction or another. Today, although certainly not as monolithic as the Catholic Church or any of the major religions, at 56 million, Taylor Swift has many times more Twitter followers than the entire Jewish population of the world.

And if Twitter followers were equivalent to citizenry, Taylor Swift would be the 24th largest country in the world (between Italy and South Africa).

UNITED STATES OF 1989

THE GOD ALGORITHM: MASTER & DYNAMIC

At the beginning of 2013, we began a relationship with a headphone start-up that is now called Master & Dynamic. The founder, Jonathan Levine, set out with the goal of making the ultimate sound company – a company that didn't sacrifice design and style in order to deliver a superior audio experience.

As we created the brand and identified who we wanted to talk to, we needed an archetype to bring the key target insights to life. We began searching for a persona that would embody appreciation for the technical superiority of the M&D product. But we wanted that persona to be more than just a technically minded person, we wanted someone who possessed boundless creativity. We needed someone we could use as a measuring stick for the work we were doing, someone who could serve as the archetypal Master & Dynamic consumer, a God Algorithm that we could filter our work through.

We found individuals who expressed unfettered genius, top thinkers and thought leaders of modernity. The kind of people the creative class reveres. Leading figures from the sciences, but also across disciplines, who demonstrated remarkable creativity and audacity, and innovative approaches to their work. One outcome of this process was "The Wall of Underappreciated Genius" at our office, where we placed people who exhibited this mindset, who could appreciate the beauty of an impeccably crafted object without relegating that craftsmanship to the world of fashion trends. The wall featured people like Bobby McFerrin, Tina Fey, Reggie Watts, Elizabeth Warren, and Dolph Lundgren. However, one man rose to the top.

Richard Feynman is an almost mythological character in the world of science. He was both a Nobel Laureate in physics and a lover of marijuana, women, and bongos. Richard Feynman found a way to experiment with LSD while still being able to make major breakthroughs in his field of study. According to one student who worked with Feynman, he was the type of person who would solve significant quandaries in physics over lunch with graduate students, not capture the proofs afterward, and leave the problem unsolved for another decade until Stephen Hawking solved it again. Needless to say, he was the person that we built our algorithm around.

"What Would Feynman Do (or Think)" was the question we asked at every stage of the game. Could we imagine our headphones as a tool in Feynman's laboratory? Could we imagine our headphones in his living room while he entertained friends? What would they need in those contexts? How could we make the "modern thinking cap," and how would we need to talk about the product to convince Richard Feynman that these were the headphones he needed? That our headphones could live up to his standards of aesthetic beauty and technical capability?

THE GOD ALGORITHM: MASTER & DYNAMIC

This persistent question, a Richard Feynman God Algorithm created specifically for the purpose of our work, acted as a guiding force for the process of creating the Master & Dynamic brand. Although we'll never have a way of knowing if we could have won over the real Richard Feynman, we'd like to imagine that the algorithm we built from the rich stories about him would have made him proud.

"NOBODY EVER FIGURES OUT WHAT LIFE IS ALL ABOUT, AND IT DOESN'T MATTER.

EXPLORE THE WORLD.

NEARLY EVERYTHING IS REALLY INTERESTING IF YOU GO INTO IT DEEPLY ENOUGH. WORK AS HARD AND AS MUCH AS YOU WANT TO ON THE THINGS YOU LIKE TO DO BEST. DON'T THINK ABOUT WHAT YOU WANT TO BE, BUT

WHAT YOU WANT TO DO."

~ RICHARD FEYNMAN

CHAPTER SIX
THE RISING MIDDLE CLASS OF INFLUENCE

Throughout much of history, influence has most often been found in two pockets — the celebrities and policymakers who distributed ideas from the very top of society and the local sense makers who interpreted these ideas and in turn told the people in their communities what to make of the ideas coming down from the top.

It was a fairly straightforward system. Some people create and distribute ideas, while others decide their merits.

In this system, immense power is placed in the hands of the few *idea distributors*. Only those with access to a "microphone" could easily get their ideas out into the world. This ability to promote ideas was almost always a matter of financial strength — land barons, kings, presidents, newspaper and book publishers, network television broadcasters all lived at the top of this model. These idea distributors created deep Influence

Wells, impacting the world around them on a large scale, and crossing still larger swathes of geography.

On the local level, there have also always been sense makers to interpret ideas. These people have been called lots of names — the influentials, the 1 in 10, community leaders, the vocal minority, and so on — but their role has always been important. Sense makers are the ones who establish values on a distributed level, and their impact on policy changes and progressive movements can't be overstated. They are the people whose minds need to be changed, as well as the mind changers. No matter what you call them — they've also been called busybodies and assholes — they are the community thought centers. The world is a complicated place, and for better or worse, we need our peers to help make sense of it all. Their Influence Wells may not be as wide as those of the idea distributors, because they often impact only the people directly around them, but there is still a deep authority in their interpretations of the world and a direct impact on the decisions of those around them.

The thing to highlight about this binary system is that it was extremely difficult for individuals to develop widespread influence outside of larger institutions. For every isolated influencer like Martin Luther, whose *Ninety-five Theses* took Europe by storm, there were hundreds of others whose attempts to disseminate their ideas outside of institutions were struck down by the power structures of the time. The arts and sciences seem to have been areas that defied this to a certain degree, but they also defied it in such a way that ideas often gained influence long after the creators had "shuffled off this mortal coil."

This system prevailed for a long time: Ideas came out into the world shared primarily by powerful distributors, and the sense makers interpreted them. Sense makers have typically been skeptical and conservative throughout history, and there is probably a deep merit to that skepticism. If society started adopting ideas before they were pressure tested, we probably wouldn't be where we are today. Of course, in hindsight, things like the Copernican Revolution seem obvious, and although we often criticize our forebears for their sluggish adoption, their prudence can just as easily be viewed as positive. If we always quickly adopted ideas from seeming experts, we might be saddled with Sir Francis Galton's eugenics or Dean Kamen's Segway, and the world would be a very different place.

AND THEN EVERYTHING CHANGED

(sorta)

The internet was born, technology became widely and cheaply accessible, and everything changed. This is so painfully obvious that it borders on the trite, and it is simultaneously so foundationally true that it can't be overstated. Everyone got a microphone.

The internet has had two major effects on the way influence works. There are assuredly an almost infinite number of changes the internet has had on influence, but here we focus on the two we see as most important for the purposes of discussing influence. The first is that it created more roles beyond just the idea distributor and the sense maker. The second is that across all the roles involved in the distribution of ideas and influence, there now exists a gradient moving from the most influential A-list celebrity down to your neighbor with 17 Twitter followers. We'll tackle these one at a time.

1. THE PROGRESSIVE ELEVATION OF CREATORS

In many ways, the model for how information is disseminated and interpreted is the same as it's always been, and the high-level roles are still the same — creators, distributors, sense makers, and the masses. What has changed, however, is the proliferation in the way that these roles are fulfilled. It's now possible to create huge Influence Wells as a creator, distributor, or sense maker, reinventing what we think influence looks and feels like. Let's look at how each of these roles has changed.

A BRIEF HISTORY OF CREATORS

In many ways, creators have seen several punctuated moments when their ability to develop and grow their influence has become more pronounced. Each of these moments had to do with the mechanisms of distribution, most recently culminating in the World Wide Web.

When Gutenberg invented the printing press, it became possible to mass produce the written word. This meant that information worthy of sharing, or at the very least, serving the agenda of some group wealthy enough to pay for a printing, became available to people on a dramatically larger scale. (Incidentally, the Bible was the first book to be printed, asking WWJD.) Over the centuries, this distribution has become more and more efficient and economically feasible. One of the most obvious and important results of this cost reduction was the introduction and widespread production of the broadsheet newspaper. These, along with the serial fiction of the "penny dreadfuls," started to bring creators to prominence on a large scale. Serial fiction in these formats gave birth to masterworks like Melville's *Moby Dick*, as well as almost all of Dickens's novels such as *Oliver Twist*, *A Tale of Two Cities*, and *Great Expectations*, to name a few.

The printing press brought Shakespeare to stages far and wide, Lord Byron's sweet nothings to the lips of lovers everywhere, and Kant's reasonings to the minds of many.

The sheer fact that we can reference their names centuries later demonstrates the level of influence that was brought to creators such as these as a result of the printed word.

In the 20th century, the emergence of broadcast radio and television increased the relevance and influence of the creators. The ability to broadcast ideas over radio gave us Orson Welles and *The Shadow*, and television amplified that ability.

From characters that defined a generation, like Henry Winkler as Fonzie, to writing and acting that helped a war-weary nation cope and understand its returning veterans like Alan Alda on

M*A*S*H, creators became an integral part of everyone's life as the role of content grew and grew.

The internet evolved the role of creators in two ways — it was the next stage in elevating the role and importance of content in people's lives, and it made it possible for everyone to share their creations easily and in a universally accessible way. This was a fundamental shift toward the "long tail" of content. It suddenly became possible for creators focused on very narrow topics to find their audience, and that audience didn't need to be in the millions. This meant that people outside the traditional machine, not beholden to the power structure of institutions, could create ideas and art and whatever else they wanted, and grow their Influence Wells without interference from those institutions' demands for profitability. No longer did influence need to be built through the help of "the man" alone. It was something that individuals could build on their own through significantly more egalitarian means.

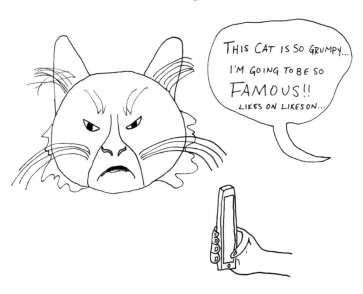

2. THE MIDDLE CLASS: DIFFUSING INFLUENCE

The second major change of the internet on the way influence works is that it has given everyone a microphone and an opportunity for their voice to be heard. Without a doubt, this has created problems in the way that information is sifted — fighting through noise and clutter is a constant struggle, and we have the "filter bubble" as a result— but it has also created a lot of positives changes. One of these is the diffusion of influence from a select few individuals at the top of a hierarchy, to a gradient of influence moving from celebrities to the average person.

We've always separated people based on their level of influence. Even in recent history before the proliferation of the internet, we classified celebrities as A-list, B-list, all the way down to Kathy Griffin. But even Kathy Griffin, regardless of how we feel about her, has a huge amount of influence compared to the average person.

Before the internet, there wasn't an easy method to bridge this gap of influence — how did someone go from average to Kathy Griffin? A lot of it was based on finding yourself in the good graces of some institution with influence (an idea distributor). If you wrote a book, you hoped it would get reviewed well in a major publication like the *New York Times*, receive some mark of approval like the Pulitzer Prize, or make an appearance on Oprah's Book Club. If you were a musician, you had to be "discovered" by some record label or their smarmy A&R guy who could distribute your art.

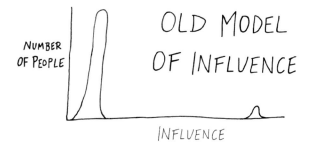

The internet changed all of this. Today, if people have something to say, they can all but completely establish themselves with a huge social media effort and a little bit of luck. In fact, this diffusion of influence doesn't even require a completely concerted effort, it can happen just as easily by accident — Antoine Dodson "Bed Intruder" and the Star Wars Kid can attest to this.

Regardless of how it happens, the important thing to point out here is that there is an immense gradient separating the average 20-something professional, and for example, some similarly aged A-list celebrity like Seth Rogen. There are now millions of people out there who don't necessarily have as much influence as Seth Rogen, but who have considerable online followings that allow them to greatly stretch their own personal Influence Wells. Influence they would almost assuredly not have without the internet.

Rob Delaney is a perfect example of this phenomena. The absurdist comedian and author of the book *Rob Delaney: Mother. Wife. Sister. Human. Warrior. Falcon. Yardstick. Turban. Cabbage.* was essentially born out of the internet like a very hairy Athena bursting from the head of a very nerdy Zeus. He has 1.06 million Twitter followers, almost perfectly in between Seth Rogen's 2.28 million and the average 30-year-old guy's couple hundred.

Historically, you were either an idea distributor on a massive scale or your influence was restricted to some region, with a city often being the high-water mark. Today, thanks to the internet, regionality is no longer a restriction for creating intermediate levels of influence. Effectively, what it's done is to create a curve, a long tail of influence, and a distribution of people between the elites and the majority of us at the bottom.

This middle class of influence is a way of distributing influence and power that has made the process of idea dissemination infinitely more complex, but (hopefully) a lot more democratic as well.

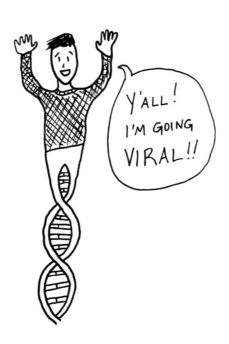

CASE STUDY

INSTAFAME

By the end of 2012, Instagram had surpassed the 100 million user mark and continued to grow at a rapid clip. Although this sort of sudden appearance and growth of a digital product was something culture was becoming more and more used to — Facebook, Twitter, Pinterest, etc. etc. etc.— it didn't come without creating social and behavioral shock waves.

In our own interactions on the platform with family and friends, we began to notice a phenomenon occurring on the Popular on Instagram tab in the app — selfies of tween and teen boys with tens and even hundreds of thousands of followers. The more we dug in, the more questions we had. Who are these teens with all of these followers? What impact are they having on the world around us? How are they changing the experience of being a teenager? What kind of power and influence do the carry? What's driving these behaviors? All of these questions were important, but the one nagging question we couldn't shake was this:

WHAT HAPPENS TO SOMEONE WHEN EVERYTHING THEY DO ONLINE IS MET WITH OVERWHELMING POSITIVE FEEDBACK?

All digital platforms on the social web have given people the opportunity to expand their network, to deepen their Influence Well, but this phenomena on Instagram felt distinctly different.

Facebook, despite its overwhelming successes, continues to strive to keep networks confined to "real" people you actually know, as does LinkedIn. Twitter offered a springboard for many, but success was demanding, requiring a lot of work to maintain and grow a following for anyone not already blessed with celebrity. But Instagram was creating micro-celebrities out of people who were posting a single photo a day, usually of themselves, with a short caption.

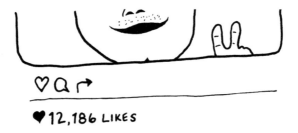

We wanted to dig into this, to experience it first-hand, and find out what this phenomenon feels like for the people at its epicenter. We wanted to understand how it's changing people and the way they perceive the world. We set out to make a short documentary that would show the world what happens on the other side of these selfies. This is when we found Shawn.

SHAWN MEGIRA

Shawn Megira is a first-generation Israeli-American who lives on Long Island. His parents' story is no different from so many

INSTAFAME

other immigrant stories. One filled with hard work, successes, failures, followed by more hard work. Shawn is the product of a loving family and a doting mother who cares deeply for her children and wants the best for them. The one key thing that separated Shawn's story from the stories of so many teenage boys was his 81,000 adoring fans on Instagram, most of whom were boy-struck teen girls.

What makes the number 81,000 so interesting is that it sits in a sort of perfect midrange of followers. A range that far outpaces the average Instagram user's reach by a considerable margin, but that is simultaneously well under the millions of followers some musicians, actors, and other celebrities possess. This middle range of followers demonstrates a middle range of influence and a middle-sized ability to affect the decisions that people make in their lives.

This is something we witnessed first-hand. In August of 2013, Shawn, along with a few of his micro-celebrity friends, decided to arrange a meetup with their fans in Times Square. They did nothing more to promote it than a few Tweets and an Instagram post with the event details, yet roughly 50 of his fans, all teenage girls, came to Times Square to meet him. These were all people he'd never met before in his life.

The reason this is significant is that it demonstrate the amount of influence Shawn has. Several of these young girls traveled from out of state to New York City just for this occasion. Not only did they have to travel themselves, they had to convince their mothers to take them on the journey. Think about this. The mere act of Shawn posting a photo with the details was enough to not only affect his teenage fans' lives, but also to convince their mothers to invest a day of their lives and $100+ on transportation to take their daughters to Time Square to spend 1 or 2 minutes in the presence of this young man. In most cases, Shawn just took a photo together with the young women and returned to talking to the friends he arrived with.

This is what the middle class of influence looks like. It also comes with a long string of strange promotions for those capable of intelligently capitalizing on it. Attending odd concerts and events to attempt to draw your fans. Promoting different small to medium apparel brands. Lots and lots of free stuff, and if you make it to the right level, financial rewards in the four-figure range for a single photo or 6-second video.

Of course, Shawn and his influence peers don't command the same kind of influence that "real" celebrities command. If Kanye West Tweeted that he was going to be in Times Square to meet fans, assuredly there would have been hundreds or thousands of his fans there to meet him. But if you were personally trying to pull a crowd of people to meet you in Time Square, and all you could do to promote it was to post a photo to Instagram and send a few Tweets, how many people do you think would show up?

SECTION THREE
APPLYING INFLUENCE

Chapter Seven
What Does It Mean For You?

Chapter Eight
Identifying Movements in Influence

CHAPTER SEVEN
WHAT DOES IT MEAN FOR YOU?

So what? TL;DR? Cut to the chase?

We get it, these kinds of books are supposed to give you some sort of applied knowledge. So let's get to that. The "what's in it for me?" conversation.

In the previous chapters, we've laid out a series of concepts that will act as foundational tools for understanding, interpreting, tracking, and applying influence.

1. INFLUENCE WELLS:
Demonstrating influence through its structural characteristics.

2. THE GOD ALGORITHM:
Exploring how individuals interpret and use mental models of influencers.

3. MIDDLE CLASS OF INFLUENCE:
Understanding that influence works on a rapidly diffusing gradient.

Each of these three tools is useful in a variety of scenarios, both for analyzing existing information and for developing strategies for building influence around a person or idea. In this chapter, we outline some more explicit instances in which you can use these models to make sense of a problem you're tackling.

1. INFLUENCE WELLS
- **Analyzing messaging**
- **Creating campaigns and initiatives**
- **Finding spokespeople and celebrity endorsers**

At its core, the concept of Influence Wells is about creating a model for what motivates people to act in certain ways. It all boils down to understanding how and why people decide to engage in certain behaviors. From our friendships to our jobs to our love lives, we're constantly trying to understand these questions. "Will she be more likely to sleep with me if I wear this shirt?" Or, "I would sleep with him if he weren't wearing so much Axe Body Spray." Unfortunately for our love lives, this tool is much more useful on a larger scale.

Whether you're creating a political campaign or a social media campaign, one of the key actions is to begin to aggregate people behind a singular message. As you build this campaign, each new person you pull in behind your cause adds a certain amount of depth to the Influence Well your campaign is building. But it's important to consider all three aspects of the Influence Well within the context of your objective — depth, breadth, and focus.

Consider the difference between a local political campaign for a congressional district and a social media campaign for Axe Body Spray.

In the case of the congressional campaign, both parties will be looking for a few things. First, they'll try to establish their message, the clarity of which will decide how focused their Influence Well is. There have been many great examples of extremely focused political messages in recent history. One of the best was James Carville's "It's the economy, stupid" during Bill Clinton's presidential campaign in 1992. Aside from its rather blunt approach, it's hard to imagine a way to keep your candidate more focused on the task at hand. All roads lead back to the economy. Every question, every debate, every interview — the economy.

This laser-like focus, the repetition of this singular message, hammered home the point that President Clinton's campaign was trying to make — we need to focus on the economy. The United States had just come out of some very tough financial years, the bottom had fallen out on the contruction trades in both '89 and '91, and we were more focused on Iraq than on establishing stability in our financial sectors. Anyone going to the polls in November of 1992 had no question about what Clinton would focus on if elected. This lack of ambiguity left no room for voters to fall out of the Influence Well that was being created in order to get people to vote for him. In more recent history, many congressional candidates in local elections have been able to create the same kind of focused message purely by saying that they'll vote against anything and everything that President Obama proposes. It's a dramatically less substantial argument, if we can even call it that, but when talking to masses of frothing talk radio listeners, it's enough.

In addition to the focus of a message, an Influence Well for a local congressional campaign also needs depth. In this case, depth is generated through the collection of influential cosigners. Of course, this can happen by bringing in established voices from outside the locale, but more effective is to bring

on board the people who mean something in that area. Certainly, if George Clooney shows up to a campaign rally in Duluth, it will probably have a positive impact. But if you have every local bartender, doctor, and minister supporting your candidate, those cosigners are going to have more influence over the voters they interact with on a daily basis. This influence to drive decision making in these cosigners' locales creates a deep Influence Well in Duluth. And who isn't looking for a little more influence in Duluth?

The final aspect of the Influence Well to consider when thinking about a local congressional campaign is breadth. In this case, what makes breadth interesting is that it's much less relevant because there is a hyper-local focus. As a candidate, you only need to focus on your congressional district, which gives you a relatively tight geographical playing field and an average size of about 700,000 people, according to the 2010 census. This means that the relevant breadth is fixed, regardless of whether you, the candidate, change your opinions or increase your credibility outside of your district. Only those people who live in your district can vote, and so that is who the Influence Well should be focused on. Each person that you reach will have an overlapping network of influence with the next person you reach, and that's OK, because you want to have potential voters feel like lots of people in their network are supporting the same candidate. However, voting is all that matters in a campaign; regardless of how the issues are debated, everything boils down to the question of which way your constituents choose to vote.

So how does this differ when compared to a social media campaign for Axe Body Spray? Other than their impact on the state of democracy, the Axe social campaign has a set of constraints that set it apart. The focus of the messaging is important in both cases, but Axe obviously has a lot more freedom to establish its message in less explicit ways. Axe isn't beholden to explicitly state, "Axe will get you girls." In fact, it's probably explicitly not allowed to say that, but it can consistently generate that message though abstract or emotional techniques. The idea that Axe will make you more manly, and as a result more attractive to the ladies, is consistent, and in this way the Influence Well that Axe generates is very focused.

In considering the breadth of Axe's Influence Well, there are two key points that separate it from a political campaign. The first is that Axe is looking for a much more specific audience, probably something like men 14 to 28, give or take a few years. This is because 14 is about the age when guys start to develop "the funk," and by their late 20s they may have moved on to more sophisticated products and smells. Although this aspect of the company's targeting narrows the breadth of its Influence Well, Axe is trying to sell products well outside of a congressional district. Axe needs to promote its relevance all across the United States and beyond. These two aspects provide clear guidelines in terms of the life stage and mindset of the people the compnay wants to influence — men in their adolescence and early adulthood — but they also create the challenge of remaining relevant across different geographies and cultures. This forces messaging to lose some of the texture and specificity a local campaign can foster — "I've been eating at Joe's since he introduced the bacon bowl!" But it allows more focus on the universality of a given experience or psychographic

— "Being a guy is smelly business."

Finally, the aggregation of influence to create depth can be dramatically more interesting and relevant in the case of a widespread campaign, such as the Axe example. Instead of choosing influencers for its geography, Axe can choose influencers based on the specific arenas in which they want to influence their target audience. This means that Axe can begin to find ways to get influencers who impact their male 14 to 28 target group. This could take the form of famous athletes who exhibit a certain caliber of style and cool like Russell Westbrook, Cam Newton, and Shaun White. It could also take the form of lifestyle icons who embody a certain type of masculinity, like Zac Efron, Pitbull, and A$AP Rocky. The idea here is to find people that these young men are influenced by or emulate, and get them talking about Axe in interesting ways in the social context. You might not turn to Russell Westbrook or Pitbull for advice on refinancing your mortgage or diversifying your portfolio, but they sure do seem to have the market cornered on looking good, and therefore also probably smelling good. When a guy in the target audience finds himself at the drugstore looking for something to abate his odor, Axe might stand out thanks to the endorsement of people he aspires to be like. This is one way of increasing the depth of the Influence Well.

Ultimately, although we developed the model as a way of better understanding influence, Influence Wells and their constituent parts form a model for analyzing communications campaigns that are built around products and ideas. They're just as relevant for social-good initiatives as they are for selling a bunch of pressurized cans of overwhelmingly potent "stink pretty." In order to use Influence Wells, you have to analyze each part — focus, breadth, depth — given the context you're working in. Here are a few key questions you should be asking as you build your Influence Well.

FOCUS: How clearly is your message driving toward a pointed and singular strategic behavior?

BREADTH: How wide a net are you casting when trying to convince people of your focused behavior, understanding that wider isn't always smarter?

DEPTH: How can you increase the likelihood of action by harnessing compelling ideas and people toward your objective?

This deconstruction allows you to find where the weaknesses lie in a campaign so that it can be bolstered before it's put out into the world. At its best, it's a means for simulating and strategically amplifying the efficacy of a campaign before it launches. At its worst, it's a post hoc analytical tool for understanding why or how something worked or didn't work. But regardless of whether it's used in advance or retroactively, the emphasis should be on whether or not the campaign is driving behavior and decisions, because ultimately this is the crux of influence — be it voting or deodorizing.

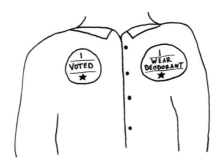

2. THE GOD ALGORITHM

- Finding influencers in a given arena
- Analyzing which spheres of influence a given person impacts

As with all of these tools, the idea of viewing celebrities through a mental algorithm was a metaphor that allowed us to understand how influence rears its head in our daily lives. But once we identified it, and realized the power of better understanding the mental machination behind why and how influencers carry their impact, it only made sense to translate that into actionable exercises.

NOW WITH ALL NEW
GWYNETH.OS
THIS IS YOUR LIFE
ON GOOP!

One of the important aspects for beginning to apply the God Algorithm is to understand what the game is. This means identifying what you believe a person stands to gain from acting on the behavior that someone else is attempting to influence them on. In any given case, understanding what a person stands to gain is the first step. Jumping back to the Goop and Gwyneth example, people are turning to her proactively because they're trying to curate a healthy, holistic lifestyle. This means that if you're selling a product, such as artisanal dirt, that might appeal to Goop's audience, you have two possible approaches. The first approach is getting Gwyneth or Goop to become a spokesperson to promote or endorse the product. This will obviously cost money, but it cuts to the chase. The second approach is to attempt to break down the Goop and Gwyneth Algorithm in order to imbue your product or brand with the values and criteria of Goop and Gwyneth. Essentially, this is a way to hack influencers — build the product directly for them.

The best place to start is with a deep analysis of the overall values and thoughts put out by a particular person, publication, or organization. You're trying to uncover where they're drawing lines in the sand in order to set criteria for your own product or brand. The goal is to use these criteria to see if your product fits with a given celebrity's or publication's ideology.

Let's break this down for Goop. The following list came from a high-level analysis of the Goop site. We've attempted to develop a systems perspective on the manufacturers of Goop, as well as taking a deep dive into a selection of their content.

POSITIVITY

Goop only shares good things. They don't critique bad things. This means that all their products are things they think are valuable. They also take this positivity to the way they approach personal growth and development. They share healthy recipes, but they don't tell you not to have your moments of indulgence. This positive-only approach is a distinct part of their algorithm.

BALANCE

There seems to be an "all things in moderation" approach. Think about others, but don't forget to think about yourself. Try this juice cleanse, but here's an amazing deviled egg recipe. Try these comfortable fashion styles, but here are some stretches to manage wearing high heels. Life's a balancing act, and Goop seems to be on board with that.

EXPERTISE

While Goop is willing to venture into the spiritual realm on occasion, they choose to do so with discussions of experts like Ram Dass. They have clinical psychiatrists talking about relationships, OB/GYNs talking about hormones and sex, and trained chefs and nutritionists talking about food. There is enough information to sort through on the internet, and by using experts Goop gains a certain level of credibility, which can ease the concerns of their readers. It gives the feeling of "we researched this, so you don't have to."

ALTERNATIVE

Whether it's through promoting "conscious uncoupling" as a way to talk about divorce or promoting aphrodisiac-infused chocolates, Goop is trying to bring the weird. Not just for the sake of it — there doesn't appear to be an ounce of irony in anything they do — but as an attempt to push the conversation about the things we think of as "normal."

This list is far from exhaustive, but it begins to illustrate the type of exercise we're talking about. What the list offers is four criteria for deciding whether or not a product fits within the algorithm the Goop-loyal are using to judge products. Does your product take an all-positive approach to the world in which it exists? Does it promote a sense of balance, avoiding the extreme margins of betterment? Does it come with a feeling of baked-in expertise and credibility from those who know what they're talking about? Does it challenge the status quo? If so, your product should, at least from a values perspective, fit into the worldview of those who are moved and influenced by the

Goddess of Goop. This means that, done right, the Influence Well your product creates should influence Gwyneth, and therefore, the Goop faithful.

This is hardly the only exercise you should go through in building a brand or product, but it's extremely useful in attempting to align your brand or product with a creative target — the aspirational audience you create for — even if it's not the only group you intend to sell to. The aim is to add texture, to breathe a larger complexity into your product or brand in order to put it out into the world with a fully formed identity.

GOOP.COM

THIS SUMMER'S TOP-5 MUST HAVES!!!

1. RAW BABY NARWHAL TEARS —
   FREE-RANGE AND MAGIC FOR YOUR SKIN

2. PIGEON FEATHER PILLOWS —
   HUMANELY HARVESTED FROM HIGHWAY OVERPASSES

3. ANTARCTIC DIRT CANDY —
   WITH 100,000 YEAR-OLD PRO-BIOTICS

3. MIDDLE CLASS OF INFLUENCE
- **Better understanding the aggregation of influence**
- **Creating larger Influence Wells through the impact of the many**

Some people are just cooler than others. Anyone who's lived through middle school has lived through the reality of that statement. But the historical model for viewing influence from a marketing, branding, or messaging perspective was, the more famous, the better. This is an antiquated concept for a number of reasons. The first reason is that, as we outlined in Chapter 6, there are more platforms and opportunities for developing varying levels of influence than ever before. This enables people to become famous and influential in narrow niches like vegan cuisine or alpaca farming. Which leads us to the second reason — influence can be aggregated by pooling the influence of a number of people toward a singular endeavor.

While pooling influence isn't always going to be the best possible solution, in most cases, when done right, it's still a strategy that creates value. However, in order to get to the point of value creation when pooling from across the middle class of influence, you have to put a lot of thought into who you want to bring together.

Early rounds of "influencer strategies" consisted mostly of giving away free stuff to people with a certain number of followers on Twitter or Instagram. Now assuredly there have been occasions when this may have worked out — everyone gets lucky sometimes. But taking a more thoughtful strategic approach is always going to pay off with higher margins.

Take, for example, our documentary work with Shawn Megira. (See the case study in Chapter 6.) Over the course of that process we found out that several companies, including Nike, had reached out and sent him free clothing. On its face, this might seem like a good idea: Send a bunch of young guys with a lot of followers free clothing in hopes they'll post images of it. The problem with this strategy was that almost all of Shawn's followers were girls. This is probably not the audience Nike was looking for to buy the clothes he was promoting.

A more successful strategy might have been to reach out to a bunch of these guys and send them men's clothes for themselves, but also send some women's apparel for friends that they'd share photos of on their stream. All of the girls who follow these young, selfie-laden Instagram streams are idealizing the guys they follow through crush behavior. This means that they're projecting their own ideals onto the guys, infusing them with the things they're hoping for in a boyfriend, which is easy because they don't actually know these micro-celebrities. If Shawn's followers are engaging in digital crush behavior, they're far more likely to emulate the girls who surround the guy they're idealizing than to go out and buy clothes for someone in their lives.

With this new understanding, we developed a four-step process that we believe to be the way to best aggregate influence.

OUR
FOUR-STEP
PROCESS

(oh yeah)

ESTABLISH BEHAVIOR

Start by understanding the behavior you want to create. Often it's something simple like voting for a candidate, or buying a specific product. But trying to wield influence without a tight, singular behavioral starting point is asinine. You need to know what buttons you're trying to push. Some larger initiatives may have multiple behaviors that need to be created. If this is the case, it's important to lay them out in sequential order. Each behavior should be approached individually.

DEFINE APPROACH

While being strategic should be part of every step of this process, defining the approach is the most strategic step. In defining your approach, you're trying to find the angle that will yield the best results. In the previous anecdote, that meant targeting popular young men's Instagram feeds to sell young women's clothing. The idea here is to uncover the category of psychological dynamics that give you an angle to drive behavior. There are the obvious fallbacks like sex, but there are ways to do this without appealing to the baser emotions. Your approach should vary depending on how complex the behavior you're trying to drive is — sex might sell fashion products, but it might not work as well selling mortgages or insurance.

IDENTIFY PLAYERS

Once you understand clearly the behavior you're creating, you then need to critically analyze the people who are influential around that given behavior, the experts or thought leaders. The alternative is to find the people who are simply influential to your target audience, independent of the given subject, and pull them into your cause. Both groups have benefits. The experts have powerful credibility that you can leverage, while the second group is aspirational to your target, but may lack credibility in the subject matter. The upside here is that since you're aggregating influence, it's possible to pull people from many different camps, developing a holistic feel through the inclusion of many different influencers.

UNIFY TEAM

The final step is to build a team out of your influencers and to get everyone "toeing the party line." There is a reason for using the political metaphor here. Most everyone can agree that although recent politicians are historically bad at accomplishing almost anything, they are spectacular at disseminating sticky ideas. This is because everyone on one side of an argument is repeating the same points. This is why the affordable care act is called Obamacare, why Benghazi was in the news for multiple seasons instead of weeks, and why there are still climate change deniers. In the case of aggregating influence, this means that all of the people you bring together need to have the same core talking points, driving toward your desired behavior.

CHAPTER EIGHT
IDENTIFYING MOVEMENTS IN INFLUENCE

When you start to think about influence as a force that impacts the movements of things in the world, as a force that all individual people and ideas possess to varying degrees and that affects those around us, you realize that it's more than just some abstraction.

Influence is as relevant for understanding and speaking about the way that a diffuse network of individuals interact and affect each other as gravity is for speaking about the movements of stellar bodies and the rotation of galaxies. Theoretically, this means that as different ideas, individuals, or entities increase or decrease in influence, keen observers should be able to see the effects of these changes in the world around them.

One way to see these changes in influence in the world around us relies on experience. When you are fully immersed in any one area, whether it's a business vertical or a personal hobby, you begin to develop a sense for who has credibility in those arenas and who doesn't. While this is probably painfully obvious, complete immersion allows a natural intuition about a subject. The problem with this way of tracking the fluctuations in the influence of something is that it's extremely time intensive, and relies heavily on the interest of the observer.

Another approach to tracking the movements in influence relies heavily on the people at the top. There is always going to be an upper echelon of influencers, in every microcosm, whose words are gospel — the most influential people who are, for all intents and purposes, infallible, permanent fixtures. The things the most influential voices are talking about will always receive an immediate uptick in influence — a rapid increase in the size of the Influence Well for whatever it is they're talking about. For example, in the world of fashion this might be Anna Wintour, Ralph Lauren, or Marc Jacobs, all gods in their own right. In the start-up world, it's people like Peter Thiel and Marc Andreessen. You can cut the subcategories ad infinitum and always find the voice that will dramatically influence the merits and weight of an idea — the voice for tracking technology adoption is Mary Meeker, the voice for sex advice is Dan Savage, and the voice for most egregious use of cheese is obviously Guy Fieri.

There is always someone at the top, and if you can talk with those people, whatever they tell you will offer you a window into which ideas or individuals are rising, and which ones are showing signs of atrophy. These experts intuitively understand the ebb and flow of influence in their fields from their constant immersion, often having completed the 10,000 hours toward becoming geniuses, as outlined in Malcolm Gladwell's *Outliers: The Story of Success*. In fact, their opinions have so much influence that even their flippant Tweets and off-hand comments can impact the course of events in their worlds. This is why we turn to Warren Buffett for every one of our business questions. He's the kindly sage of modern business.

But what happens when changes are so subtle, so fluid, or so fast that even the standard bearers aren't necessarily in tune with what's happening in a way they can express? To get to these deeper, longer story arcs of influence, you need to undertake immersion on a holistic scale — history, aesthetic, consumer sentiment, adjacent industries, etc. From our perspective, there are three major methods for these explorations, things that we go through when we try to uncover how influence is impacting a category we hope to innovate in.

1. Look Backward To Look Forward

2. Articulate The Unspoken

3. Feel It

1. LOOK BACKWARD
TO LOOK FORWARD

When trying to figure out what the future holds, the most obvious and oft-used means of exploration is to take a step backward and understand how a category has gotten to the place it finds itself in today.

It makes sense. There is no great intuitive leap in looking backward when attempting to uncover the threads of meaning that weave together to build some larger cultural tapestry of tomorrow. The leap comes in the ways and places we choose to look.

The best analogy for this process comes from star gazing. When you find yourself lucky enough to be looking up into a clear sky on a dark evening, the sheer volume and variety of stars in the sky can be breathtaking. And amid all of the bright constellations — the Big Dipper, Orion's Belt, and Cygnus — there are these tiny little specks of dim light that are just barely visible. You know they're there, so you stare straight at them, but thanks to the shortcomings of the human eye, you can't see them. The cones at the center of the human field of vision, our retinas, are far less light sensitive than the rods on the perimeter. However, if you look just a little off center, those almost invisible stars appear. And suddenly you're catching a glimpse of something small, something lost in the sea of information around it, but that is absolutely real even if it's not easy to see.

Uncovering the thread of influence and finding meaning and significance for the future is exactly like this. Staring directly at the thing you want to learn about is going to offer you only so much. If you want to find meaning, you need to look all around, but not directly at the thing you want to understand. You need to see all the disparate and separate information that surrounds it, both close in and far out, and all of the sudden the thing you've been looking for pops into view in the corner of your eye.

AN ANALOGY IS WORTH 1,000 WORDS

One way we attempt to find meaning when uncovering movements in influence is to use close-in analogies and success stories. These case studies act as bits of information that are proven and accepted, and, like the constellations, they have been seen by a billion other people, and interpreted in a million different ways. The interpretation of these analogies is actually the beauty of this exercise. When looking at case studies that people have looked at a billion times, turning your head a little to the left can make all the difference.

For example, people constantly look to Apple as a fount of inspiration. It is the quintessential story used to demonstrate the value of having a visionary leader, and more often than not draws a "duh" and an epic eye roll. Great. We get it. Steve Jobs. It's been used so much it's lost meaning.

But if that is the only thing we can learn from Apple's success story, we are being hopelessly myopic — navel gazing instead of star gazing. Looking more closely, what we might find is that the intense secrecy of the internal Apple projects generated a culture that perpetuated a feeling of importance and insider status among employees. That a little secrecy can go a long way to connect people around a shared vision. The point is that there are definitely deeper learnings to be found even in the most overused and clichéd case studies. It's just a matter of taking a step back, cocking your head, and choosing to look at the skies a little bit differently.

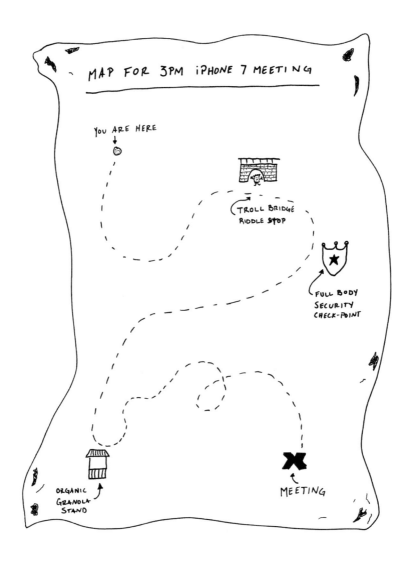

LOOK EVERYWHERE ELSE

The other way to identify the movements of influence when it seems like meaning won't present itself — like looking for a dim star in a sea of bright ones — is by looking somewhere else entirely. This can often mean finding and ascribing meaning to seemingly all but irrelevant examples in the world— like examining the Irish potato famine to understand corporate monoculture. Dig deep into psychology journals, history books, philosophical treatises, comics, cartoons, music lyrics, and art — anywhere you can find inspiration.

Simply having a concept to unpack and trying to tie it to a curious problem can be enough to find the hidden meaning in something. Because there is something intrinsically human about influence, the spark of understanding a problem can just as often take the form of pop culture or fiction as it can academia. Pop culture and fiction can be extremely useful windows into the way that people think and proxies for understanding what people are and aren't ready for — fundamentally the most important aspect of innovation.

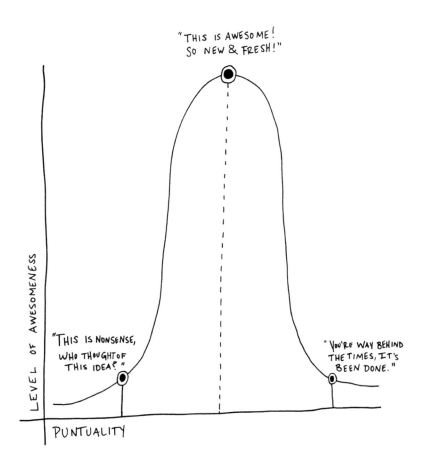

AT ITS SIMPLEST, <u>OPTIMUS TIME</u>™ IS THE WINDOW OF TIME WHEN FORCES ARE ALIGNED FOR THE IDEAL INTRODUCTION OF A NEW BEHAVIOR, PRODUCT, OR IDEA.

2. ARTICULATE THE UNSPOKEN

Another exercise we go through when trying to uncover movements in influence is simply unloading all of the observations we have gleaned during immersion. All of them. The whole enchilada. No observation left behind.

What we've learned is that people, ourselves included, are really bad at realizing the import, value, or relevance of something that hasn't been clearly articulated. Our team will sit down and write about things without any clear direction, with no idea of what we need to say. The exercise is the writing itself.

This idea works in the same way that journaling through a difficult experience works. When counselors or psychologists recommend journaling to their clients, it's not because they're trying to set them up to sell their memoir, it's because sometimes you can't know what you know or how you feel until you put it into words. Thoughts are inherently nebulous, the stuff of emotions and fleeting sparks, understanding without saying. Words are rational and concrete, the stuff of communication, the things that birth our ideas into the real world. Writing your ideas down acts like an anchor.

When you go out into the world and investigate problems, it's easy to take certain observations for granted — to pass over observations as givens, knowns, things that are already part of the collective body of knowledge. However, in reality, very little fits into this "givens" category, and in order to build toward bigger, bolder, and more complex ideas it's important to put the givens down on paper. Because if something is a given, truly a given, you still need to be able to account for it in the way that you're building your model of the future, as one more piece of the puzzle.

The way to grapple with givens is to think of them like individual blocks in a structure you're building. If you have 150 Legos, you can build something that is recognizable as the object you're trying to recreate — be that the Millennium Falcon or Santa Claus. But if you have 15,000 Legos, the amount of detail and complexity you can build into that Millennium Falcon is increased exponentially. In both cases, what you've built is a Millennium Falcon, but by increasing the number of blocks you're building with you can dramatically increase the resolution of the information you're conveying with the model. Most of the time, you can't build big ideas without the little ideas.

And in keeping with this metaphor, it's not uncommon for us to take a huge amount of our writing and cut it up into discernible chunks in order to put it back together into something larger and more meaningful. This isn't a metaphor. We actually print out Word docs or Excel sheets, cut them with scissors, and physically build bigger ideas from the little ones. By grouping ideas according to their relevance to each other, sometimes called affinity mapping, the relationship between all the bits of information presents itself. This is an incredibly helpful exercise in coalescing bigger ideas out of the tiny thought fragments that we have floating around in our heads.

Because of this, we put as many ideas down as possible. Throw everything out there on the table. Volume is good. The act of simply putting our thoughts, ideas, and observations down into words formalizes them; editing can come later. Value judgments of ideas are easy once the ideas exist. Getting them out is often the hard part, and so often we just forget to say the things we're thinking. We don't always use this method, but contrary to popular belief, sometimes quantity can breed quality.

3. FEEL IT

We've already said this, but it bears repeating. We're firm believers in intuition, and in the ability of our guts to solve problems before our minds can.

This means that when things feel right, more often than not there is a reason for it, even if it's not the reason we think. And when things feel wrong, there's probably a really good reason for that too. You can't trust your gut without doing the work to support it, but you have to start somewhere, and intuition is a great place. This is ultimately the foundation of the scientific method — identify a hypothesis and test it.

Human beings are incredibly well-tuned sensation and perception machines, and this includes our ability to sense veracity in ideas. Harmony has a feeling. It's something we can hear and viscerally respond to when listening to music, but it extends beyond that. There is a feeling you get when you look at a math problem that has the correct answer, you can sense the harmonic beauty of it. When you see 1+1=2, you can feel the rightness.

That same feeling applies when looking at something as complicated as forecasting the future by using influence. In fact, it's even more valuable, because you're going to have to trust the way ideas feel before you dig into them. Because while showing your work is just as important in this case as it is in solving math problems, your intuition can save you a lot of work. Intuition is your protection against the need to solve problems with brute force, or even worse, following bad ideas down dead ends.

This is the least satisfying of the three characteristics of projecting influence in terms of its tangibility, but it's also the most human. The more people do things, the better they get at them, and the easier it is to make the intuitive leaps of insight. Intuition is the product of a practiced hand, it's the coalescing of all of our experiences. And most importantly, it happens automatically if we're thinking critically. It may be the least satisfying of the three, and also the most often overlooked, but it's probably the most valuable.

"THE ONLY REAL
VALUABLE
THING IS

INTUITION"
~ALBERT
EINSTEIN

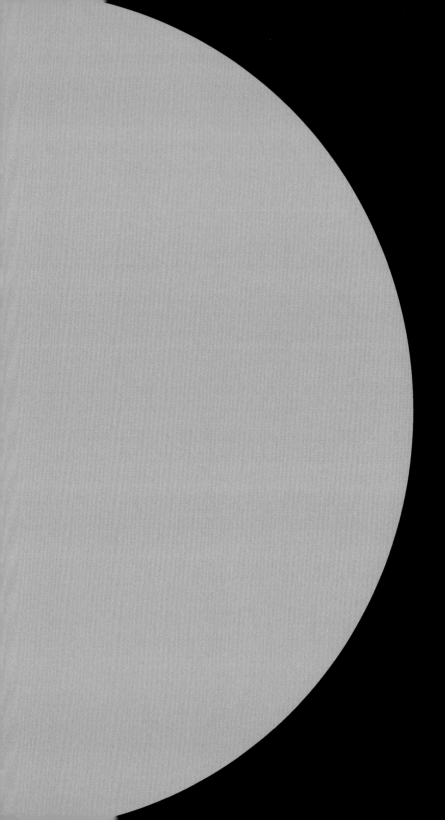

SECTION FOUR
WRAPPING IT ALL UP

Chapter Nine
Why Did We Write This Book?

CHAPTER NINE
WHY DID WE WRITE THIS BOOK?

How do you feel now that you've finished this book? Like youe life has just changed? Like you're quickly going to take over the universe? Like you'll lead with an iron social graph, and Mark Zuckerberg will be the patron saint of your realm? That's great. This is exactly what we were hoping to accomplish.

Just kidding. Our goals were much more humble than that.

This book is a treatise on approaching seemingly boring or ultra-jargony questions in a really human, and maybe even occasionally humorous, way. Because it's so much easier to learn when you're enjoying the process. It's something we all inherently know, but occasionally forget. There is no need to take ourselves so seriously.

Because we were constantly being asked questions about influence, very earnest questions, we decided to write a book about it. However, we wanted to write a "business book" that didn't make you want to rip your hair out. Bring a little bit of "real talk" to the business world. All of you know that you could benefit from a bit more real talk — we certainly know we could as well. For better or worse, sometimes real talk involves discussions of Gwyneth Paltrow's latest trends in bowel movement management. We don't make the rules.

By bringing a bit of "real talk" to some questions that marketers are actually asking, we are going to help make the business world ever so slightly more human. And then someone else is going to find a way to do it much better than we are. This is how things work. Humanity is always getting better as a whole, one step at a time. Whether it's someone setting a seemingly unbreakable record only to see it broken shortly thereafter, or it's someone compounding information learned from others to hit an even greater mark. This is our verse to be contributed to the world of business books — as if the world were asking for that — and you too can contribute a verse.

Maybe you're reading this book on a plane cruising over Toledo or in a crowded quiet car on the Acela Express somewhere on the beltway, and you're smiling while reading. You get to work and you make some bizarre connection between this year's futuristic looks at the Met Gala and their impact on the adoption of digital personal assistants, or the relationship between the number of selfies a person takes and their audience engagement based on age. That is what success looks like for this book. That would make us wildly happy. (It also sounds really cool, please share that report with us.)

We wrote this book because we wanted to help people draw connections between seemingly irrelevant bits of information to build a larger view of the world they live in, but more importantly, a more fun and interesting view of that world. We wrote this book to encourage others to connect the dots that people aren't really paying any attention to. To braid together the thinner threads to form stronger ideas in the world.

We also wrote it because it tickled us. If you made it this far, maybe it tickled you too. If you think that this is just a bunch of pseudo-intellectual self-indulgence, we're more than ok with that, as long as you had fun.

We're more than happy to settle for giving you a good time.

Thanks for reading our book.